Caged Poet's

escape diary

Pranshu Patel

/ BookLeaf
Publishing
India | USA | UK

Made with ❤ on the BookLeaf Publishing Platform

www.bookleafpub.in

www.bookleafpub.com

Dedication

To all the unheard , unloved and people who were
victims of conditional love.

Preface

This book was never meant to be published it was simply a collection of feelings, scribbled between pages of a diary. But sometimes, a gentle push changes everything. My journey as a poet began two years ago, and six months back, I gathered the courage to share my first poem on Instagram. It didn't reach many, yet it reached one of my dearest friend, whose encouragement breathed life into these words.

One person's belief was enough to turn quiet thoughts into verses, and verses into this book.

I owe my deepest gratitude to my best friend, my family, and my online companions whose warmth and support carried me through this journey. Their faith in me helped these poems find the light of day.

"Caged Poet's Escape Diary" is a collection born from raw, unfiltered emotions, poems about self-love, the heaviness hidden in love, unconditional affection, and everything in between. I hope you find a reflection of yourself in these words, and that each poem whispers something your heart has been longing to hear.

In the end, I wish for you the purest gift life can offer 'the love you truly deserve', unbounded and unconditional.

Acknowledgements

I would like to express my deepest gratitude to all those who guided and supported me to all those who guided and supported me throughout this journey.

Firstly, I would like to thank bookleaf publications, who helps poets like me to share all the unsaid and unspoken words and phrases into poems.

Secondly, I would like to express my deepest gratitude to my bestfriend, family members and my online friends whom I had deep conversations with. I would like to appreciate the people who helped me gain experience to jot them down into poems.

I owe my deepest gratitude to every heart that has ever whispered a word of kindness my way.
To those who taught me that silence can speak, and chaos can create your lessons live between my lines.

To my family, who became my first audience and my forever home;
to my friends, who believed in my voice when I was still

learning to listen to it;
and to every stranger whose story touched my soul
thank you for being the poetry behind my poetry.

This book is not mine alone it belongs to every tear,
every laugh, and every late-night thought that shaped
these words.
With love and endless gratitude.

~ Pranshu Patel

1. Beautiful Betrayal

I was fed love on silver spoon,
everyone believed, everyone envied;
"She is so lucky", they said,
" I wish I were her ", they felt.

A sharp knife positioned on my spine
was so hideous no one noticed;
Love is a blessing, they say,
no one mentions the cons it comes with.

I was never fed I guess,
I was made to choke on love;
Love to me has always been a *golden cage*,
or a Devil dressed so nice pretending to catch me by
surprise.

Love was a drug to me,
it was withdrawn when I disobeyed;
"Oh to be loved ", they said,
Alas unconditional love is non existent.

Love is a barter, an unfair trade,
I had to trade my energy;
The golden child they mention,

I suffered on the so called pedestal.

Favorite of everyone, hated by none,
forced to be a people pleaser, pleased by none;
Deep down I know, I would be thrown,
when useless, I would be forgotten.

2. If I turned into a worm

Walking in the garden, holding dear's hand,
The fragrance of flowers following us;
His charming smile ugh, makes my heart flutter,
His eyes, I saw affection for me.

Suddenly hit a thought, what if I turned into a chrysalis?,
Would I be loved if the misery happened?;
Would I be adored? would I be cared for?,
heart paused a for a bit, brain urged to carry on the
thought.

No hands, no legs, no brain would I be loved despite
that?,
No sense of humour, no sarcasm would I be loved in
spite of that?;
What if I can't give him what he needs?
Would I be adored despite being useless?

Suddenly thought of a mischievous scheme,
I would offer him a worm, to recognise his thoughts;
Picked a worm, asked him for his hand,
Placed it on his hands, "this is all yours now" I said.

He giggled, confused, "okay" he said,

Take a good care of him, I mentioned;
We headed back then, thought about worm all the time,
Wondered what would he be doing?

Went to his home thinking then,
He welcomed me with smile;
"What's the worm doing?" I asked,
"Look to your right" he replied.

Saw a little plant in a pot, didn't notice that worm,
"It became a chrysalis" he mentioned;
"Soon will become a butterfly and he will fly",
" Won't you be sad if it flies off?" I asked.

" I would be, but it's his life" he replied,
With a smile, I got reassurance;
I would still be loved, still be adored,
I hold him tight, thinking I would still be loved if I were
to be a worm.

3. Semisolid

Met my grandpa last week,
Had a great chat, had fun talk about past;
We laughed, giggled,had a great time,
He paused for a bit, " I have an advice.

"Be like semi-solid" , he said,
Not soft enough to spill;
Not hard enough to shatter,
Just enough of both, makes you little better.

Learn to hold yourself together,
When the world presses too close;
Don't bend, don't break,
Just stay, and learn to let go.

Don't be like liquid,
For you'll bend, even when it is not meant;
It's okay if something rejects you,
No need to just vanish.

Don't be like solid,
For you will break, when given lot of pressure;
Just adjust a little, adapt a bit,
Things would be just fine.

Live in the middle,
Between power and pleasing;
Be something what suits the situation,
Be unpredictable, hideous your cards.

And that's what dear, my advise for your life,
I have lived enough, learned better;
And yes my child, never forget,
Be like semi-solid.

4. Winner takes it all ?

"The winner takes it all " they say,
the praises, the approval makes the day;
Oh to be the spotlight , the only one,
the champion hated by none.

The glory , the fame , the height,
I suppose why does everyone fight?;
A little more grind , a bit more hustle,
I wonder why they all bustle.

I suppose victory is misleading,
Then why does it seem so eye pleasing?;
Don't ask the one who envies,
Ask someone who owns trophies.

The shining gold medal, felt heavy on my chest,
Misery hidden in luminiesced;
Eyes full of jealousy, pretending to be happy,
Suffocates me, makes me feel crappy.

Victory was expected, dear ones not surprised,
I did it for love, I suppose, I despised;
Kept winning just to be taken granted for,
The losers had what I endured for.

Everything I needed was on the ground perhaps,
Everything I earned is worthless perhaps;
In the end looser envies winner, winner envies looser,
One is loved despite that , one is unloved in spite of that.

5. Unnoticed

Everyone mentioned love, Alas I had nothing to say,
I was the least favorite toy of the child;
Or was the last child at adoption center,
Perhaps was the last person whom they asked to play.

The people, never heard my name;
my stories, never mentioned on dinner tables;
Silence and solitude described me best they said,
I never wanted that no one knew.

The quiet kid, easy to handle,
Less chaos, most obedient;
Neither loved , not hated,
Just *Unnoticed.*

Always a *lover,* never the *beloved,*
Always the last grain left on plate;
Never noticed difference between love and attention,
To be noticed felt like affection.

I envy them, the chosen ones,
they were noticed, were loved ,were pleased;
The *golden children*, got everything,
Us *unnoticed,* were overshadowed.

They were adored for being something,
The empty ones were just nothing;
Perhaps in other universe,
I won't remain *Unnoticed*.

6. My other life

Humans can't be defined, we are a spectrum,
Then why is she so secretive, about her *other life*?;
Perhaps she doesn't want to mix her two lives,
Or, she doesn't want to be called a double face.

Family would hate her chaotic side,
My friends they dislike her stoic side;
She despises mixing her both worlds,
Them knowing her other side would make her suffer.

She is chaotic, but she is stoic,
She is clumsy, yet she is responsible;
Yes, she can be both, however she hides,
"I dislike showing my cards", she says.

I don't want to be understood,
I don't want any misunderstanding either;
Being known, is like being naked,
Being known, would make me used, she feels.

It's not a pretense, she is being herself,
She just hides, likes the comfort;
People don't need to know everything,
A little secret won't hurt anyone.

This is what everyone does,
Not showing cards, is not bad idea I guess;
Humans can't be defined, we are a spectrum,
No one needs to know, about *My other life*.

7. Coffee date

Went for a walk today,
followed road to the *past;*
Guess who I ran into by the way?
Younger me finding way to west.

Asked her for a *coffee date,*
She agreed , we went to an old place;
She asked for a latte and cake in plate,
" one americano please "I asked with grace.

"You changed a lot it seems " she was mentioning,
" I had no option " I responded;
She said I looked calm but compelling,
"Thanks to you" I said we giggled;

"Some advice from the future?", she asked,
Don't pretend to be strong;
Little girl was confused,
Being vulnerable is not wrong;

I had lot to tell, a lot to express,
A lot to advise, a lot to console.
I paused, it would be no fun then,
I thought, journey is better than destination,

" You are a smart girl" I replied to her,
"you will figure things out yourself" I added;
Knowing less is far better,
Suddenly everything faded.

I woke up , my brain felt fogged,
I rubbed my eyes , guessed it was a dream;
Put my feet on the ground and streched,
I wish I could do that by crossing a brim.

8. Perfectly imperfect

In a world full of imperfect people,
Why chasing something so non-existent
Why becoming fool birds, chasing endless horizon,
Perfection is a myth, chasing it is a curse.

Look for perfection in imperfection instead,
It is beautiful to love ordinary;
How pretty everything seems,
When rain drops feels like pearls dropped from sky.

When wrinkles resonates waves in the sea,
Or when moles seems like stars in the night sky;
There is a reason why rose has thorns,
There is a reason why deer have horns.

There is a reason for all the chaos,
The same reason why you are imperfect;
Chasing perfection is a trap, wake up people,
You don't know you are *perfectly imperfect*.

9. High walls

To protect the pure soul *oh* I,
Tried to build *my walls* too high;
Instead of fixing the broken boundaries,
I broke and rebuild them.

Again and again, strong to stronger,
construct them till no one can break;
Lost the thieves, who wanted to break in,
What's the point of having people then.

If all they have is bad intentions,
All those trying to scratch my walls;
I attack them with arrows, pull them away,
The threat to my soul, was threat to my life.

Kept on doing what I did,
Even if I had to abandon beloved;
Being alone suddenly felt safe,
Solitude gave reassurance, people failed to give.

kept people who adored me with my space,
Cherished my boundaries, never tried to break walls;
But, was it really worth it??,
Maybe I forgot what I wanted to protect.

10. Solitude

In the world so crowded,
I felt peace being alone;
Too many fishes in the sea,
But I was in love with the shore.

Where whispers of the waves complain,
And grains of sand, my only throne;
Beneath the sky, a canvas grey,
I found my heart in tranquil mores.

The salt-kissed breeze a gentle balm,
As seagulls dance and spirits soar;
In *solitude*, I found my calm,
In quiet thoughts, my soul restored.

Crowds suffocate me, *solitude* brought peace;
Amidst the chaos, my heart's release;
With every rustle of the leaves,
I breathed in whispers, forged my beliefs.

Here, time drifts like drifting tides,
Unraveled thoughts on moonlit rides;
In every sigh of ocean's breath,
I found my life, where silence met.

11. No is not a bargain

No is not a bargain, it's a choice,
No is not a trade, it's is my voice;
I said it because I felt like so,
My consent matters just like yours, you know.

No woman is a machine, we are humans too,
We need rest and our opinions matters too;
I screamed, I pleaded, can't you hear man,
Listen to others, you pea brained man.

No means I stand firm, I won't bend or break,
No isn't a puzzle for you to remake;
My thoughts are not yours to carve and mold,
I'm not here to fit in your stories you've sold.

I don't want love, if it's negotiation,
I don't want this type of conversation;
No is not a bargain, it's a choice,
No is not a trade, it's my voice.

12. Extraordinary curse

You say you love roses, but can't bear thorns;
You say you love the rain, but complain about its cons;
You say you love the breeze, but hate when it makes you sneeze;
You say you love me, but dislike when I speak.

Everyone likes beautiful things,
None likes the flaws coming.
It's no one's fault not being loved,
No one's fault having flaws either.

Only a mighty soldier who loves peace
Won't mind a war first.
Guess I was not hard to love
Maybe never found a soldier.
Only a farmer values rain; the ordinary can't love the precious.

Don't downplay, don't feel unlovable, a soldier like me is waiting for someone.
18 years of life, one lesson learnt:
Being alone is better than being blamed for thorns.

To every rose reading this: having thorns ain't your

fault,
It had a reason to exist, it exists to protect the precious.

Cherish your thorns; don't let ordinary have you.
A soldier doesn't mind bleeding, the ordinary would cut
them all.

So it's either waiting and cherishing,
Or losing and mourning.
The choice is yours,
Precious honey, please pick the soldier.

13. Eyes that feel

Everyone tries hard to search *eyes that feel,*
A soul that understands and listens;
Where can I find someone like that?,
Do these type of people exist?

Eyes wandered, searching for the one,
Diving into the souls, found no empathy;
My heart aches now, burnt out my soul,
Can't find the one, I want to vomit my thoughts.

Picked up my diary, and painted my words,
Bleed down thoughts till, the heavy burden on heart fell
off;
it was a long journey till I,
Figured out it was me, myself and I.

The lost valuable I was seeking was right under my nose,
I never noticed I was a feeler myself;
The empathy I searched for was in me,
I am the *eyes that feel.*

14. Not lonely

In a room full of croud, I am alone,
Not lonely, just missing you;
The commotion and attention,
Makes me wander into your thoughts.

I urge myself, to look for someone else,
Thinking about you makes me pause;
Your absence keeps my company then,
I'm not missing you, I just don't want to miss you.

How clueless are you?,
I find you by myself;
What more clues do you need,
Alas, you can't hear me far away.

15. Drowning person

A pleasant morning, of coming spring,
I went to popular lake, to watch the scene;
I was near the lake preparing for boating,
Went into the lake, it was so clean,

Enjoying fishing, I saw a person,
Fell into the lake not knowing how to swim;
Rowed the boat near him, his situation worsen,
I threw a rope into water to save him;

The guy was almost dizzy, was unable to help himself,
I intended to help him out;
Intuition gave me a warning, a harm on yourself,
However, I gave my hand to bring him out;

The hand hold on to me tighter,
Pulled me into the water;
The person pressed my head into the water,
I drowned going deeper and deeper,

Eyes felt blur, I woke up scared,
Heart beated fast, what was that?, said to myself;
I realised it was an illusion so bad,

Sigh! I guess that was a sign not to save again a *drowning person.*

16. Escape

When storms began to crowd my sky,
And every dream forgot to fly,
I packed my silence, left my pain,
And walked away through pouring rain.

The voices called, I didn't turn,
Their lessons tired, too much to learn;
The city hummed its endless plea,
But I was done, I chose to be.

No map, no plan, no grand goodbye,
Just fading echoes, soft and shy;
Sometimes you don't need strength to stay,
Sometimes escape is the brave way.

So let them say I ran away,
They'll never know the price I pay;
For peace was hiding past the fight,
And I found freedom in the night.

17. Animals giving life lessons

Birds are so fool ,
flying to the horizon which doesn't exist ;
Ants are stupid,
getting stuck in non-existent.

Dogs are morons ,
going back to people who hurt them ;
Cats are silly ,
hiding their feelings.

Oh wait doesn't it seem a bit familiar,
Maybe I have seen it somewhere;
These patterns are haunting me,
Reminding my wrongs.

Perhaps it was when I was working hard,
Burning my happiness for a cheerful future ;
Alas, I found it late,
Life is short, why delay the joy.

Maybe it was when, following non-existent rules,
I would have been happier breaking;
Silly me chose to be a follower,

I regret I kept on doing so.

I kept going back to heartbreaker dear ones,
I sealed my mouth to keep the beloved;
I did it wrong, I realised it later,
I'll thank the pea brained animals for such *life lessons*.

18. Woman have it easy, really?

Victims card holders, pretty privilege,
No financial burden, privileged laws ;
Girls have it easy, women are biased,
Men's money, women get it all.

The little girl's so confused,
it was nothing it seemed to be;
Blamed for wearing revealing,
Blamed for not sitting properly.

Blamed for going out at night,
Blamed for not cleaning mess others made;
Blamed for not earning the same,
Blamed for working too long.

Blamed for being heavy weight,
Blamed for being too skinny;
Blamed for looking attractive,
Blamed for looking unattractive.

Blamed for being housewife,
Blamed for being working women;
Blamed for having kids,

Blamed for not having kids.

Privileged laws ain't helping,
blaming the victim instead;
looking at it makes the little girl wonder,
Do women really have it easy?

19. Journey is better than destination

Hustle hard , relax later ,
Everything will be fine then;
All this pain is worthy,
Of the better future, they say.

What would I do if I achieved?,
What will I do if I have what I yearned for?;
Silence, peace and no stress,
Is that what I always wanted?.

I find happiness in chaos,
Hope in struggle;
Strength in perseverance,
And myself in the *journey.*

How would I hate the path?,
Can't hate the mirror;
Who shows me reflection of myself,
My scars, the spark in my eyes.

The tough times were familiar routine,
Each day was a mystery;

After reaching the Happy ending I can say,
The journey is better than destination.

20. Rome wasn't build in a day

Rome wasn't build in a day,
Neither the urge of leaving home;
The warm , cozy and comfort place,
Seems like a cage to her.

The hot and cold behavior,
Suffocates her, feels like living death;
She is caged by affection,
The betrayal is wrapped in care.

The heart urges to break the cozy cage,
And free the wanderlust spirit;
The mirage of comfort and warmth,
She don't want it all.

She gets silenced by silver and gilded life,
You are nothing without money they say;
The roots don't allow the tree to grow,
The cat denies the kitten to go.

One day I will break those chains,
She hopes, she urges, she yearns;

I will have my own silver,
The name, fame and a home.

21. Season 18

Dear diary, season 18 of my life happened,
I'm confused, curious, clueless just not confident;
I envy the privileged, the rich, the sorted,
Want to be them, keeping this words unsaid.

life gives me lessons, I can't understand,
everyday, I hope I can be perfect;
I want to be appreciated, for I tried my best,
Golden years, they say, nothing golden it feels.

Some say enjoy, some say hustle,
How am I gonna balance it all?;
I fear I'll miss out (FOMO),
I'm anxious, can't help.

All these back stabbers, make me so upset,
Oh, I wished people liked me more;
No results I wished for, I get my ego crushed,
Alas, *season 18* of life happened.